crochet your own
merry and bright baubles

Kati Gálusz

becker&mayer! books

Brimming with creative inspiration, how-to projects, and useful information to enrich your everyday life, Quarto Knows is a favorite destination for those pursuing their interests and passions. Visit our site and dig deeper with our books into your area of interest: Quarto Creates, Quarto Cooks, Quarto Homes, Quarto Lives, Quarto Drives, Quarto Explores, Quarto Gifts, or Quarto Kids.

Published in 2020 by becker&mayer! books, an imprint of The Quarto Group, 11120 NE 33rd Place, Suite 201, Bellevue, WA 98004 USA.
www.QuartoKnows.com

This book is part of the *Crochet in a Day: Crochet Your Own Merry and Bright Baubles* kit and is not to be sold separately.

becker&mayer! books titles are also available at discount for retail, wholesale, promotional, and bulk purchase. For details, contact the Special Sales Manager by email at specialsales@quarto.com or by mail at The Quarto Group, Attn: Special Sales Manager, 100 Cummings Center Suite 265D, Beverly, MA 01915 USA.

20 21 22 23 24   5 4 3 2 1

ISBN: 978-0-7603-6951-7

Library of Congress Cataloging-in-Publication Data available upon request.

Author: Katalin Gálusz
Design: Kate Sinclair
Photography: Chris Burrows
Editorial: Meredith Mennitt
Production: Yuhong Guo

Printed, manufactured, and assembled in Shenzhen, China, 05/20.

Distributed by:
Quarto UK, The Old Brewery
6 Blundell Street, London N7 9BH, UK
Allen & Unwin
30 Centre Rd, Scoresby VIC 3179, AUS

MIX
Paper from responsible sources
FSC® C017606

Image credits: All stock photographs and design elements © Shutterstock

#340616

Contents

About This Kit

This kit contains the tools and materials you will need to make a colorful ornament: yarn in yellow, magenta, green, pink, blue and purple; an E/4 (3.5mm) crochet hook; a needle; and stuffing.

How to Read the Instructions

Every line starts with the round/row number in bold, and ends with the stitch count in parentheses.

Instructions in square brackets must be repeated the specified number of times before continuing with the remaining instructions of the round or row (if any).

Abbreviation Chart

BO	BOBBLE STITCH
CH	CHAIN OR CHAINS
DC	DOUBLE CROCHET (US) TREBLE CROCHET (UK)
RND	ROUND
SC	SINGLE CROCHET (US) DOUBLE CROCHET (UK)
SL ST	SLIP STITCH
ST	STITCH OR STITCHES
YO	YARN OVER

Notes on Tools and Materials

YARN

The pattern in this book was designed with DK (light worsted) yarn, but you could use any yarn thickness: as long as you stick to it throughout, and choose a matching hook, your ornaments will turn out just as fine, only smaller or bigger than the original.

HOOK SIZE AND GAUGE

Exact gauge is not important in this project, as long as you work tight enough to create a fabric that doesn't gape too much when you stuff the ornament. To achieve this, you will need a hook size smaller than recommended on the yarn's label. The balls featured in this pattern were crocheted with E/4 (3.5mm) hook, but this is only a guideline; feel free to experiment to find what best suits your crocheting style.

STUFFING

I recommend polyester fiberfill, as it is easily available and economical, and makes resilient, washable projects.

If your gauge was a bit loose and you are worried that stuffing might escape between stitches, you might use a piece of tulle or other light fabric (for example the toe of nylon stockings) to make a pouch that will safely contain the fiberfill. Alternatively, instead of stuffing you could use a styrofoam ball, or a cheap christmas bauble - these have the added bonus of making the ornament's shape perfectly round too. Depending on the size of the bauble/foam ball, you might need to add or remove a round or two of the crochet halves, to ensure a snug fit.

Crochet Stitches and Techniques

This chapter contains a short primer on the techniques you will need to create the ornaments, but if you are new to crochet, I suggest to practice the basics before starting the actual project. Many yarn shops offer classes, or you can look up video tutorials online.

SLIPKNOT

Use this to begin a chain, or a standing stitch. Make a loop on your yarn a few inches from the end. *(Fig. A)* Insert your hook through the loop and grab the yarn end connected to the skein. Pull the strand through the loop, then tighten the knot. *(Fig. B)*

MAGIC RING

The magic ring is a nice technique to start working in the round, because it will create a small circle of stitches with no gap in the center.

Make a circle of the yarn. Insert your hook through this ring *(Fig. C)*, YO and draw up a loop *(Fig. D)*, then ch 1. Work the first round of stitches over both the ring and the free yarn end, then pull on the free end to close the ring.

YARN OVER (YO)

Wrap the yarn around your hook from back to front.

CHAIN (CH)

Make a slipknot first, unless you are in the middle of a piece and already have a loop on your hook. YO, and pull yarn through the loop on hook. Repeat as many times as required. *(Fig. E)*

The loop on the hook doesn't count as chain, so omit it if you are checking the stitch count.

WORKING INTO STITCHES

Every stitch has two strands in a small V shape on top. Insert your hook under both sides of the V unless otherwise specified.

WORKING INTO A CH-SPACE/BETWEEN STITCHES

Most of the stitches in this pattern are worked either into chain-spaces, or into the gaps between dc stitches, rather than into the stitches themselves.

SLIP STITCH (SL ST)

Insert your hook into the st or ch, YO and pull yarn through both the st or ch and the loop on hook.

SINGLE CROCHET (SC)

Insert your hook into the designated place, YO and draw up a loop (pull yarn through st or ch). You will have 2 loops on your hook. YO and pull yarn through both loops on hook. *(Fig. F)*

DOUBLE CROCHET (DC)

YO, insert your hook into the designated place, YO and draw up a loop (you will have 3 loops on hook). *(Fig. G)* YO and pull through 2 loops on hook, then YO again and pull through the remaining 2 loops on hook.

BOBBLE STITCH (BO)

The pattern uses the 3-dc version of the bobble stitch.

*YO, insert your hook into the designated place, YO and draw up a loop. YO and pull through 2 loops. *(Fig. H)* Repeat from * twice, inserting your hook into the same place. *(Fig. I)* YO and pull through all 4 loops on hook. *(Fig. J)*

STANDING STITCHES

Standing stitches are used when joining a new color. You always start with a slip knot, then make the stitch exactly the same way as normal stitches within the round.

STANDING SC

Make a slip knot with your new color. Insert your hook into the designated place, YO and pull up a loop (you will have 2 loops on your hook). YO and pull through both loops on hook. *(Fig. K, L & M)*

STANDING DC

Make a slip knot with your new color. YO and hold the yarn with your forefinger. Insert your hook into the designated place, YO and draw up a loop (you will have 3 loops on hook). YO and pull through 2 loops on hook, then YO again and pull through the remaining 2 loops on hook. *(Fig. N, O & P)*

STANDING BOBBLE

Make a slip knot with your new color. YO and hold the yarn with your forefinger. *YO, insert your hook into the designated place, YO and draw up a loop. YO and pull through 2 loops. Repeat from * twice, inserting your hook into the same place. YO and pull through all 4 loops on hook. *(Fig. Q & R)*

RIGHT & WRONG SIDE

If you are working in rounds without turning, there will be a right and a wrong side. The right side is the side facing you while you work; this should be the outside of your piece.

FASTEN OFF

To fasten off, cut the yarn 3-4 inches from your hook (or more, if you will need the yarn end for sewing), and pull the end through the last loop on the hook.

WEAVE IN YARN ENDS

In this project, the yarn ends will be on the inside of the balls, so it is not necessary to weave them in. But if you want to make sure they won't show up between stitches, you can thread them into a needle one by one, secure them by stitching through several st on the wrong side of the piece, then snip off the rest close to the crochet fabric.

Materials

- 7 YARDS (6.5 M) OF YELLOW WORSTED WEIGHT YARN
- 7 YARDS (6.5 M) OF MAGENTA WORSTED WEIGHT YARN
- 12 YARDS (11M) OF BLUE WORSTED WEIGHT YARN
- 13 YARDS (12M) OF GREEN WORSTED WEIGHT YARN
- 13 YARDS (12M) OF PINK WORSTED WEIGHT YARN
- 13 YARDS (12M) OF PURPLE WORSTED WEIGHT YARN
- 0.5 OZ (14G) OF POLYESTER FIBERFILL
- E-4 (3.5MM) CROCHET HOOK

Finished size: ~3" (80 mm) round

Instructions

Each ornament consists of two identical halves (though you could certainly pair two different sides, for an even more colorful ball!) For every round, you will join a new color with a standing stitch and fasten it off with a slip stitch at the end of the round.

COLOR ARRANGEMENTS

The yarn in the kit is enough to make any one of these three color plans. You can of course make up your own color sequences instead - but please note that you might run out of a color if using it more heavily than in the original arrangements.

PLAN A	PLAN B	PLAN C
1. Yellow	1. Magenta	1. Pink
2. Magenta	2. Pink	2. Purple
3. Green	3. Purple	3. Blue
4. Pink	4. Yellow	4. Yellow
5. Blue	5. Green	5. Green
6. Yellow	6. Pink	6. Magenta
7. Purple	7. Purple	7. Pink

ROUND 1

Make a magic ring, then ch 3 (counts as a dc). *(Fig. A)*

Dc 11 into the ring. *(Fig. B)* Pull the ring tight, then sl st into the top of the ch-3. *(Fig. C)* Fasten off (12 dc, no ch-spaces).

A

B

C

ROUND 2

Starting with a standing bobble with your new color, work [bo 1, ch 1] into each gap between the dc of rnd 1. *(Fig. D & E)*

Sl st into the first bobble and fasten off (12 bobbles and 12 ch-spaces). *(Fig. F)*

Check the magic ring - you might find that it went loose and needs to be tightened again.

D

E

F

ROUND 3

Starting with a standing dc using your new color, work 3 dc into every ch-space. *(Fig. G & H)*

Sl st into the 1st dc and fasten off (36 dc, no ch-spaces). *(Fig. I)*

G

H

I

ROUND 4

Starting with a standing sc with your new color, *sc between the first and second st in any of the 3-dc groups. *(Fig. J)*

Ch 1. Sc between the second and third dc of the group, ch 1. *(Fig. K)*

Skip the space between the 3-dc groups. Repeat from * 11 more times. *(Fig. L)*

Sl st into the first sc and fasten off. (24 sc and 24 ch-spaces)

J

K

L

ROUND 5

Starting with a standing dc with your new color, work 2 dc into every ch-space. *(Fig. M, N & O)*

Sl st into the first dc and fasten off (48 dc, no ch-spaces).

ROUND 6

Starting with a standing sc with your new color, *sc between the stitches of any 2-dc group, ch 1, skip the gap between the 2-dc groups. *(Fig. P)*

Repeat from * 23 times. *(Fig. Q)*

Sl st into the first sc and fasten off (24 sc, 24 ch-spaces). *(Fig. R)*

ROUND 7

Starting with a standing sc with your new color, work [sc 1, ch 1] into each ch-space. *(Fig. S)*

Sl st into the first sc and fasten off (24 sc, 24 ch-spaces). *(Fig. T)*

Make another identical piece for the other side of the ball, but when fastening off after Rnd 7, leave a long yarn end (about 18") for sewing.

Optionally, weave in the short yarn ends on the wrong side of the pieces. Then align the two halves, wrong sides together, and sew them together. *(Fig. U)* Pause when you have about 1" opening left, stuff the ball, then finish the sewing. *(Fig. V)*

HANGING LOOP

To make a hanging loop, cut about 12" of any color you prefer. Pull it through under the seam and tie the ends together. *(Fig. W)*

Great job! Enjoy your Merry & Bright Baubles!

#CrochetInADay

About the Author

KATI GÁLUSZ discovered the world of amigurumi when she wanted to make a unique gift for a toy-collector friend. What started as a quick fling has grown into the love of a lifetime, allowing her to combine her need for creativity with her two main interests, animals and great books and movies. After lavishing her creations on her long-suffering family and friends, she started to sell them on Etsy and share her crochet patterns on Ravelry. When she is not crocheting, she can be usually found with a book in her hand, surrounded by her dogs in her home near Budapest, Hungary.

crochet
IN A DAY

crochet your own
reindeer ornaments

INCLUDES:

- 32-Page Instruction Book
- 5 Colors of Yarn
- Crochet Hook
- Yarn Needle
- Fiberfill
- Safety Eyes